SUPER CUTE!

Baby
WOLVES

by Bethany Olson

BELLWETHER MEDIA • MINNEAPOLIS, MN

Note to Librarians, Teachers, and Parents:

Blastoff! Readers are carefully developed by literacy experts and combine standards-based content with developmentally appropriate text.

Level 1 provides the most support through repetition of high-frequency words, light text, predictable sentence patterns, and strong visual support.

Level 2 offers early readers a bit more challenge through varied simple sentences, increased text load, and less repetition of high-frequency words.

Level 3 advances early-fluent readers toward fluency through increased text and concept load, less reliance on visuals, longer sentences, and more literary language.

Level 4 builds reading stamina by providing more text per page, increased use of punctuation, greater variation in sentence patterns, and increasingly challenging vocabulary.

Level 5 encourages children to move from "learning to read" to "reading to learn" by providing even more text, varied writing styles, and less familiar topics.

Whichever book is right for your reader, Blastoff! Readers are the perfect books to build confidence and encourage a love of reading that will last a lifetime!

This edition first published in 2014 by Bellwether Media, Inc.

No part of this publication may be reproduced in whole or in part without written permission of the publisher. For information regarding permission, write to Bellwether Media, Inc., Attention: Permissions Department, 5357 Penn Avenue South, Minneapolis, MN 55419.

Library of Congress Cataloging-in-Publication Data

Olson, Bethany.
 Baby wolves / by Bethany Olson.
  p. cm. – (Blastoff! readers. Super cute!)
 Audience: K to grade 3.
 Summary: "Developed by literacy experts for students in kindergarten through grade three, this book introduces baby wolves to young readers through leveled text and related photos"– Provided by publisher.
 Includes bibliographical references and index.
 ISBN 978-1-60014-934-4 (hardcover : alk. paper)
 1. Wolves–Infancy–Juvenile literature. I. Title.
 QL737.C22O473 2014
 599.773'139–dc23

                                                        2013003491

Printed in the United States of America, North Mankato, MN.

Table of Contents

Wolf Pups!

Baby wolves
are called pups.
They are born
in **litters** of
four or more.

Life With Mom

Their mom is the **alpha female** of the **pack**.

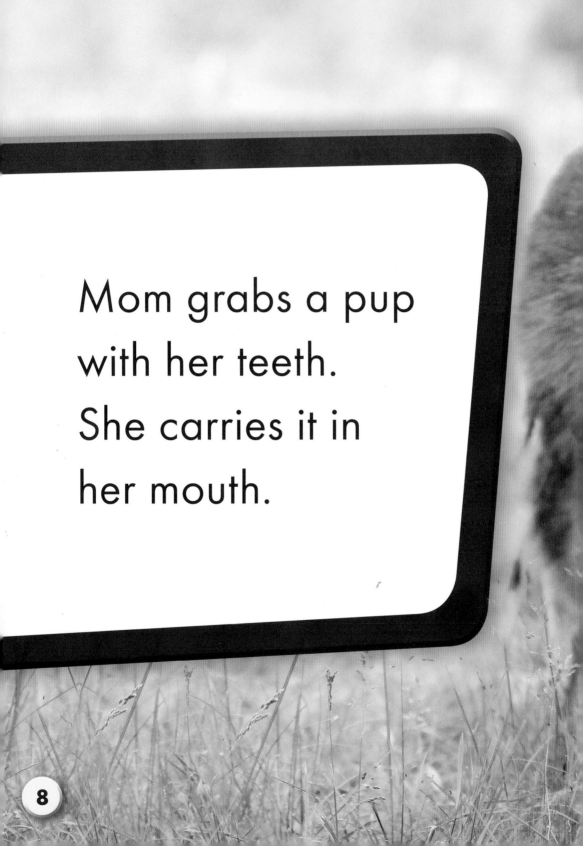

Mom grabs a pup with her teeth. She carries it in her mouth.

The pups nap
with mom.
They like to
snuggle when
they sleep.

Mom feeds her pups. **Newborns** drink her milk. Older pups eat from her mouth.

Mom teaches her pups to hunt for **prey**. Then they feast together.

Playtime

Pups explore with one another. They run and climb outside their **den**.

Pups also **wrestle** for fun. Soon they will fight for their place in the pack.

Pups **howl** to call to the pack. This sound can travel many miles. Awoo!

Glossary

alpha female—the female wolf that leads a pack along with the alpha male

den—the place where wolf pups are born and raised

howl—to make a long, loud cry

litters—groups of babies that are born together

newborns—babies that were just born

pack—a group of wolves that live together

prey—animals that are hunted by other animals for food

wrestle—to fight in a playful way

To Learn More

AT THE LIBRARY

Askani, Tanja. *A Friend Like You*. New York, N.Y.: Scholastic Press, 2009.

Doudna, Kelly. *It's a Baby Gray Wolf!* Edina, Minn.: ABDO, 2008.

Marsh, Laura. *Wolves*. Washington, D.C.: National Geographic, 2012.

ON THE WEB

Learning more about wolves is as easy as 1, 2, 3.

1. Go to www.factsurfer.com.

2. Enter "wolves" into the search box.

3. Click the "Surf" button and you will see a list of related Web sites.

With factsurfer.com, finding more information is just a click away.

Index